The Type that is Not for Me

By

Willson Adam

Chapter 1: The Myth of "My Type"

Theme: Debunking Romantic Patterns

Introduction: The Type Trap

We all know *that* type. Tall. Funny. Wears black. Writes poetry. Or maybe it's someone ambitious and mysterious—emotionally unavailable but devastatingly charming. "He's just my type," we say, grinning sheepishly, as if those excuses everything. But here's the kicker: *our type is often a trap*. Not because attraction is wrong, but because many of us unconsciously build patterns based not on joy or compatibility—but on wounds, fantasy, and social programming.

E. Jean Carroll, with her razor-sharp humor and fearless honesty, invites us to look directly at those patterns and ask: **Who taught you to want what you want?** Did you choose your "type," or did your past shape it? Did culture sell you a checklist that never served you? Have you confused attraction with chaos, or chemistry with drama?

This chapter is about demolishing the idea that there is only one kind of person for us. It's about setting fire to the myth of "my type" and stepping into the glorious unknown of what real, soul-level connection could look like—when it's not confined to a curated fantasy.

Section 1: Who Told You What to Want?

Let's start with this uncomfortable truth: many of us didn't invent our "type." We inherited it. Through movies, books, early crushes, trauma bonds, or unmet childhood needs, we built a romantic ideal that—ironically—has little to do with love. We crave what's familiar, even if it's painful.

Maybe your type was:

- The bad boy who disappears when you need him most.
- The intellectual who loves ideas more than intimacy.
- The fixer-upper who shows "potential" if you just pour yourself dry to build him up.
- The emotionally distant, enigmatic one who keeps you guessing.

These patterns aren't just *personal*—they're *cultural*. We're taught to chase the mysterious, the dangerous, the aloof. We're taught that passion is suffering, and that "working for someone's love" means we've earned it. But what if you don't have to audition for affection? What if what you've called your "type" is actually your trauma trying to rewrite its ending?

Section 2: Patterns Masquerading as Preference

There's a difference between *preference* and *pattern*. A preference says, "I like someone kind, curious, and confident." A pattern says, "I keep falling for people who make me feel invisible—but I swear this one's different."

Your type often starts as a preference and then hardens into a blueprint. Soon, you find yourself rejecting good, stable people who don't fit the mold. You friend-zone healthy options and romanticize chaos. You equate butterflies with emotional danger—but still crave the rush. And before long, *your type becomes your cycle.*

Here's how to tell when "your type" is harming you:

- You keep getting hurt by similar kinds of people.
- You romanticize red flags ("He's just complicated.")
- You ignore your values in the name of attraction.
- You feel drained, anxious, or unworthy in your pursuit of them.

As Carroll would say: Stop chasing people who don't even *like* themselves. And for heaven's sake, don't call self-abandonment chemistry.

Section 3: Journal Reflection

Prompt: Who was "your type" in the past—and why?

Take a moment to reflect.

- What traits did they have? (Looks, style, job, hobbies?)
- What did they *make you feel*—initially and eventually?
- Where did this "type" come from? (Media? Family dynamics? A need to prove your worth?)
- What parts of yourself did you have to shrink to be with them?

✍ Write freely below. Don't censor yourself. Name the type. Own it. Expose it.

Section 4: Exercise — The "Type" Breakdown

Let's break the fantasy. On one side, list all the qualities you've historically thought you *needed* in a partner. On the other, label each trait as either:

- ✅ **Authentic** (truly aligned with your core values)
- ✖ **Performative** (impressed others or felt expected)
- ⚠ **Harmful** (led to emotional pain, confusion, or compromise)

Quality I Thought I Needed	Category	Why I Chose It (Be Honest)
Witty & sarcastic	✅ Authentic	Humor is my love language and helps me feel alive.
"Dark and mysterious"	⚠ Harmful	I confused aloofness with depth.
Super successful	✖ Performative	I wanted to prove my worth by being chosen by status.
Emotionally unavailable	⚠ Harmful	Familiar from childhood—felt like love.
Artist with a tortured soul	⚠ Harmful	It seemed romantic—but it was exhausting.
Gym-obsessed & muscular	✖ Performative	Looked good on Instagram, but didn't connect with me.
Kind and communicative	✅ Authentic	I crave emotional safety and real connection.

Once you finish this list, **draw a line through every performative and harmful quality**. It's time to retire those patterns.

Section 5: The "Type-Free" Dating Manifesto

What if your type…was a dead end?

What if, instead of seeking a *type*, you opened yourself up to *a person*?

A person who made you feel safe, seen, celebrated—not someone who just matched your aesthetic or your wounded inner child's craving for approval. When we abandon the false comfort of types, we make space for *discovery*—and that's where the magic is.

"Love doesn't always come in the package you expected. But it will feel like freedom when it's real."

— Inspired by E. Jean Carroll's irreverent clarity

Section 6: Writing Prompt — A Type-Free Vision

Prompt: What would a "type-free" approach to dating or relationships look like for you?

Imagine this:

- You're sitting across from someone who isn't your "usual."
- They don't meet your checklist.
- But they make you laugh until you cry.
- They remember small things about you.
- They don't play games.
- You feel like *yourself*—fully.

How would that change your story?

✍ Write about it. Envision it. Get curious.

Let go of the packaging, and tune into the presence.

Section 7: Homework — Dating Outside the Box

Whether you're single or partnered, this is your challenge:

Break one pattern this week.

- Swipe right on someone you normally wouldn't.
- Say yes to a friend's setup even if "he's not your type."
- Reflect on someone who treated you well—ask yourself why you dismissed them.
- Compliment someone's energy, not just their looks.

📓 Journal the experience. How did it feel to step out of the mold? What surprised you?

Section 8: Conclusion — Rewrite the Ending

You are not doomed to repeat romantic cycles forever. You are not bound to your "type" like a script you can't edit. The truth is, *you get to write a new story*—one where love feels safe, fun, rich, and real. But first, you must give up the myth that your type knows best.

Let E. Jean Carroll's boldness be your guide. Laugh at the patterns. Burn the checklist. And remember: being open to someone unexpected may be the most rebellious, romantic act of all.

"Darling, he may not be your type—but maybe *your type* is what got you here in the first place."

— Not My Type Workbook

Chapter 2: Ghosts of Bad Boyfriends Past

Theme: Breaking Up with Your Romantic History

Introduction: Enter the Ex-Files

We all have one (or several). The man who made you question your worth. The one who ghosted. The one who "just wasn't ready" after two years of emotional investment. The manipulator. The user. The charming destroyer of peace. And let's not forget the infamous gaslighter—fluent in blame-shifting and void of accountability.

E. Jean Carroll's *Not My Type* teaches us that it's not just about moving on. It's about reclaiming the pieces of ourselves we handed over to the wrong people. This chapter is about more than forgetting an ex. It's about exorcising them. Clearing out the residue of their dysfunction from your confidence, your standards, your identity. It's time to look at those relationships not through the lens of nostalgia or regret—but through power, humor, and clarity.

So grab your shovel. We're digging up some ghosts—not to mourn them, but to bury what never should've been resurrected.

Section 1: The Real Cost of Loving the Wrong People

Let's get honest: love isn't always lovely. Especially when it chips away at your self-esteem, makes you doubt your instincts, or teaches you to normalize the unbearable.

Bad relationships don't just break hearts. They can:

- Reshape how you see yourself.
- Reinforce self-doubt and people-pleasing.
- Settle you into a comfort zone of emotional chaos.
- Make you feel like love is supposed to hurt.

And it's not just the heartbreak—it's the *aftershock*. Months (or years) of second-guessing your worth. Wondering what you did wrong. Shrinking yourself so it doesn't happen again.

But what if the lesson wasn't about *you being too much or not enough*—what if the only mistake was trying to make a home in someone else's emotional war zone?

Section 2: The Greatest Hits of the Worst Exes

Let's take a tour through the ex-boyfriend hall of fame. See if any of these ring a bell:

- **The Ghoster**: Vanishes mid-conversation and reappears when Mercury is in retrograde.
- **The Critic**: Always had "feedback" about your outfit, your friends, your laugh.
- **The Commitment-Phobe**: Wanted all the benefits of a relationship without calling it one.
- **The Project**: You saw potential. He saw a free therapist, chef, and life coach.
- **The Manipulator**: Made everything your fault. Gaslit you into apologizing for his failures.
- **The Placeholder**: Never saw your worth, just feared being alone.

You loved them, yes. But did they love *you*, or the way you made them feel?

Were you their partner—or their emotional crutch?

Section 3: Journal Reflection

Prompt: Write a "thank-you, next" letter to an ex who derailed your confidence.

This isn't about bitterness—it's about liberation. Write to that person who made you question your beauty, your value, your voice. Don't sugarcoat it. Don't protect them. Tell the truth. Then release it.

Your letter should cover:

- What they did that broke you.
- What you tolerated.
- What you've learned.
- What you're reclaiming.
- A fierce goodbye.

Example Opening:

Dear [Insert Ghost's Name Here],

I used to think losing you was the worst thing that happened to me.

Now I see it was the beginning of my freedom.

You made me doubt my worth. I made excuses for your absence, defended your coldness, and silenced my needs to keep the peace. I stayed loyal to the version of you I made up in my head.

But here's the twist—I'm not sorry anymore. I'm *grateful*. Because your love starved me so thoroughly, I had no choice but to feed myself again.

Thank you, next. I hope someday you meet someone who demands more of you than I ever did.

Goodbye forever,

Me

Section 4: Exercise — Red Flag Bingo

Goal: Identify your personal pattern of ignoring deal-breakers disguised as "quirks."

Draw a 5x5 bingo grid or use the example below. Mark every red flag you've tolerated. When you get a full row, column, or diagonal—congrats! You've survived a toxic romance.

Emotionally Unavailable	Love Bombed Then Withdrew	Didn't Apologize	Made You Feel "Crazy"	Constant Ex Talk
Lied About Small Things	Avoided Labels	Breadcrumbed You	Controlled Your Clothes	Bad Listener
Passive-Aggressive	Gaslit You	CENTER: "Not Ready"	You Played Therapist	Withheld Affection
Dismissed Your Feelings	Turned Friends Against You	Had a Backup Plan	Rushed Intimacy	Ignored Boundaries
Criticized Your Body	Gave Backhanded Compliments	Never Planned Dates	Was Jealous But Distant	Emotionally Draining

✍ Reflection Questions:

- Which red flags did you ignore most often?
- Where did you learn to normalize these behaviors?

- What would it look like to choose someone who *doesn't need you to rescue them?*

Section 5: Prompt — What Did You Put Up With That You Now Find Outrageous?

Hindsight isn't just 20/20—it's often hilarious *and* horrifying.

Think back to past relationships and ask:

- What did I explain away?
- What did I pretend didn't hurt?
- What did I lower my standards for?
- What did I mistake for love?

Examples:

- Waiting three hours for a text back—and still replying with a smiley face.
- Driving to his house even though he never came to yours.
- Laughing at jokes that hurt your feelings because "he didn't mean it."
- Apologizing for crying during an argument *he started*.

📝 **Write a list. Make it raw. Make it ridiculous. And then underline the ones you'd *never* tolerate again.**

Section 6: Release Ritual — Let the Ghosts Go

It's time for a symbolic breakup with the past.

 Here's your ritual:

1. Write your ex's name(s) on a piece of paper. Add the emotional weight they carried: "Guilt," "Shame," "Unworthiness."
2. Tear it up or burn it (safely). Say out loud:

"I release this story. I reclaim my power. I do not belong to this pain anymore."

3. Dance it out. Seriously. Move your body like you're shaking off years of ghostly residue.

 Play your best "I'm too good for you" playlist while you do it.

Section 7: The Lesson Is In the Leaving

Some of the best things that ever happened to us were the people who *left* us. Or the ones we finally had the courage to leave.

You don't need to find meaning in their mistreatment. You only need to find your way back to yourself.

Let them be part of your past—not your narrative. You don't owe their memory a pedestal. You owe yourself peace.

"Darling, it's not your job to rehabilitate emotionally stunted men. Let their next girlfriend enroll them in therapy."

Section 8: Affirmations for the Post-Ex Era

Repeat these as you rebuild:

- I do not mistake chaos for love.
- I trust myself to recognize what is safe, kind, and true.
- I no longer romanticize people who do not respect me.
- I am no longer available for love that drains me.
- I am grateful for every exit that led me back to myself.

Conclusion: From Ruin to Rebirth

They were wrong for you. And maybe you were wrong for you back then, too—unknowingly choosing from pain, scarcity, or habit. But that version of you made it through. And the you reading this now? She's the hero of the story.

As E. Jean Carroll would say: *"Don't just get over him. Get fabulous."*

So here's to ghostbusting your love life. To laughing at the heartbreaks that once leveled you. To raising your standards so high the wrong ones get altitude sickness.

The ghosts are gone. Let's build something real.

Chapter 3: The Real You is Not Up for Debate

Theme: Radical Self-Acceptance

Introduction: You, Unedited

Let's get one thing straight: *you are not a pitch.* You're not a product, a profile, or a performance designed to be liked. You are not a PowerPoint presentation in a push-up bra. You are not an algorithm trying to increase your chances of being swiped right on. You are a *person*—and that, in all your messy, brilliant wholeness, is enough.

This chapter is about peeling off the layers—what you do to please, to be chosen, to be adored—and asking: Who am I when I'm not editing myself for anyone?

E. Jean Carroll never begged to be understood, accepted, or adored. She knew that the most powerful, magnetic thing a woman could be was **herself**, full-stop. And that's exactly what we're going to reclaim here: the courage to exist without apology.

Section 1: The Performance of Being Lovable

Let's be real: from a young age, women are taught to curate themselves. To adjust volume. Smile more. Don't be too needy. Don't be too cold. Be sexy, but not *too* sexy. Be smart, but don't *intimidate*. Say you love sports, even if you just came for the snacks.

So you start shape-shifting:

- Laughing at jokes you don't find funny.
- Nodding in agreement when you actually want to scream.
- Becoming "cool girl," "chill girl," or "fixer girl"—roles you never auditioned for but got cast in anyway.

Eventually, it becomes second nature. You dress for the fantasy. You shrink for approval. You date like a contortionist, twisting yourself into someone you hope he'll keep.

But what if the real tragedy isn't that they didn't love you—but that you didn't show them *you* in the first place?

Section 2: What Radical Self-Acceptance Really Means

Self-acceptance isn't:

- Reciting affirmations while secretly believing you're not good enough.
- Settling for loneliness in the name of independence.
- Posting a bikini pic and calling it empowerment while secretly hoping for validation.

True self-acceptance is:

- Letting yourself be visible without seeking permission.

- Not shape-shifting to fit someone's expectations.
- Choosing yourself *even if*—especially if—no one else claps for it.

"I love myself. That's the beginning of a lifelong romance."

— Oscar Wilde (and probably E. Jean Carroll's morning mantra)

To accept yourself radically is to stop arguing with your own existence. It's not about arrogance—it's about refusing to shrink for the sake of being chosen. Because here's the wild secret: *when you stop trying to be lovable, you become irresistible.*

Section 3: Journal Reflection

Prompt: Who are you when you're not trying to be lovable?

Take a moment to write uncensored answers to these questions:

- How do you dress when no one's looking?
- What do you say when you're not worried about being liked?
- What brings you joy—not performative joy, but bone-deep pleasure?
- Who are you when you're not auditioning for affection?

📝 Write it out. Let it be messy, funny, defiant, emotional. This is the version of you who deserves the world—not just romance, but *recognition.*

Section 4: Exercise — Rewrite Your Dating Profile (Even If You're Not Dating)

This is not about apps. It's about *owning your narrative*. If you wrote a dating profile—or even a life mission statement—from a place of **radical self-like**, what would it say?

Here's the challenge:

You're not trying to be cute, agreeable, or impressive. You're trying to be *truthful*. What would you write if you believed your presence was the gift?

☐☐ Use this template and fill it in *as outrageously, honestly, and unapologetically as possible.*

Name:

Queen of Owning Her Story (but you can call me [Your Name]).

About Me:

I laugh loudly, love messily, and have a PhD in calling out bullshit (mostly my own). I'm not here to audition—I already got the role. I believe in books over brunch, deep conversation over small talk, and being worshiped like a goddess *or else*. I've cried in the car, danced in my kitchen, and healed myself so many times I've lost count.

My Superpowers:

- Making people feel safe enough to tell the truth.

- Walking away from things that dull my sparkle.

- Making playlists that feel like therapy.

Dealmakers:

- Kindness. Humor. Curiosity.

- Emotional fluency (or at least a willingness to learn).

- Energy that says "I see you," not "How can I use you?"

Dealbreakers:

- Performers who want the vibe, not the responsibility.

- People who confuse control with care.

- Anyone who says "You're too much." (I'm not.)

Final Thought:

I'm not looking to be completed. I'm looking to be met. If you can't handle depth, don't swim here.

Now you try. 💅 Go wild. Go deep. Go *you*.

Section 5: Prompt — What Makes You Magnetic Beyond Appearance or Approval?

Beauty fades. Approval shifts. But *you*—when you're centered and in your truth—are pure magnetism.

Write out your non-physical superpowers:

- Do people feel safe around you?
- Do you speak truth without sugar?
- Do you make others laugh until they can't breathe?
- Do you hold space for grief, growth, and glitter?

📝 **Write a list titled "I Am Magnetic Because…"**

Let it roll out like gospel. This is your essence, not your aesthetics.

Section 6: Mirror Work — Say It Like You Mean It

Find a mirror. Look into it. Say these things out loud:

- "I am not on trial."
- "I am not a puzzle to be solved."
- "I am not responsible for making others comfortable with my fullness."
- "I will not be quieter, smaller, or simpler just to be palatable."
- "I am already enough."

Do this for seven days. Watch what shifts.

Section 7: Permission Slip to Take Up Space

Here's your permission slip, signed by E. Jean Carroll in spirit:

💌 **You have full permission to:**

- Be too loud.
- Take selfies for *yourself.*
- Cut people off mid-gaslight.
- Laugh at your own jokes.
- Cry at the dinner table.
- Say "I deserve more" without apology.
- Date people who make you feel like Beyoncé in a crown, not Cinderella scrubbing floors.

Tape it to your mirror. Or better yet, tattoo it on your soul.

Section 8: Real Self, Real Standards

Radical self-acceptance doesn't just feel good—it changes *everything*. When you stop negotiating your worth:

- You stop explaining your boundaries.
- You stop dating potential.
- You stop chasing closure, affection, or half-hearted people.

You start being alone without being lonely. You start enjoying your own company like it's a five-star affair. You stop asking, "Am I lovable?" and start saying, "Am I being loved in a way that honors me?"

That shift? That's where the miracles happen.

"Be the kind of woman who doesn't have to announce she's the prize. Just carry yourself like you know it."

Conclusion: You Are the Standard

This isn't about self-help. It's about **self-truth**. The real you—the one who's felt too big, too emotional, too honest, too much—*is not up for debate.*

You don't owe anyone an explanation for your needs, your voice, your heart. And if someone doesn't get it? Bless them and block them.

Let E. Jean's fire remind you: You were never supposed to be agreeable. You were supposed to be *unforgettable.*

So take up space. Love your quirks. Stand in your power. And remember: the real you is the only one worth falling in love with.

Chapter 4: Stop Being Nice, Start Being Honest

Theme: Unlearning People-Pleasing

Introduction: Niceness is Overrated

We've all been raised in the Church of Niceness. Praise be to politeness, sacrifice, and staying likable at all costs. We learned that being "nice" keeps the peace, earns approval, and protects us from judgment. But here's what they didn't tell us: **being nice can ruin your life**.

Being "nice" can keep you in relationships long past their expiration date. Being "nice" can silence your no. Being "nice" can make you say yes when your soul is screaming no. It makes you bite your tongue, laugh when you want to cry, and agree when your gut is in open rebellion.

E. Jean Carroll didn't become an icon by playing nice. She became unforgettable by being honest, sharp, and unapologetically herself. This chapter is about shedding the mask of agreeability and learning to choose *honesty over harmony*.

Section 1: The High Cost of Being "Nice"

Let's define the difference:

- **Nice** is performative.
- **Kind** is intentional.
- **Honest** is holy.

You can be kind and direct. You can be compassionate and firm. But "nice"? "Nice" is often a lie dressed in pearls.

Let's talk about what niceness has cost you:

- Time spent nodding through boring dates.
- Silence in the face of cruelty because you didn't want to "cause drama."
- Smiling through discomfort just to be liked.
- Saying yes to a third date with a man who made you feel like a warm plate of wallpaper paste.

"Nice" doesn't get you intimacy—it gets you invisibility.

"Nice" doesn't get you respect—it gets you resentment.

Niceness is not your virtue. It's your muzzle.

Section 2: What's Beneath the People-Pleasing?

People-pleasing is a survival strategy. Somewhere along the way, many of us learned that love must be earned. That approval must be performed. That safety is linked to obedience.

You might be a people-pleaser if:

- You apologize for things you didn't do.
- You say yes, then feel drained, bitter, or overwhelmed.
- You avoid conflict like it's contagious.
- You value being liked more than being real.
- You try to be "easygoing" even when everything inside you is shouting.

This isn't about judgment—it's about liberation.

Because here's the truth: You don't need to earn being loved. You don't need to win the room. You don't need to over-explain, over-apologize, or under-function just to be tolerable.

You are allowed to take up space. You are allowed to disappoint people. You are allowed to say what you mean, without a thousand disclaimers.

Section 3: Journal Reflection

Prompt: Where has "being nice" kept you silent, stuck, or small?

Answer the following prompts:

- A time I said "yes" when I meant "no":
- A moment I stayed in a relationship/friendship because I didn't want to "hurt them":
- A conversation I avoided because I was afraid of being seen as rude:
- A boundary I watered down to keep the peace:
- A time I smiled when I wanted to scream:

Now ask yourself:

- What would I have said or done if I had trusted my honesty more than their comfort?

Let the answers come raw and loud. This is where your real voice begins.

Section 4: Practice — Write Your "Hell No" Texts

Let's take your power back one message at a time. Below are some real-life scenarios where you might be tempted to say "maybe" when you mean "hell no."

Instructions:

Choose 3–5 examples from the list below and write a direct, respectful, and clear message that says **no**—without apologizing for it.

SCENARIO 1: The guy who keeps texting "WYD" at 11:47 PM.

Old you: "Haha not much, just chilling."

New you: ???

SCENARIO 2: A friend who always makes everything about them but never asks about you.

Old you: Listens for hours, then cries alone later.

New you: ???

SCENARIO 3: Someone asks for a favor you *really* don't want to do.

Old you: "Sure! Of course!"

New you: ???

SCENARIO 4: You're asked on a second date, but you know there's no spark.

Old you: "I'll let you know!"

New you: ???

SCENARIO 5: You're invited somewhere out of obligation.

Old you: "I guess I should go."

New you: ???

📝 Now, write your new responses.

Example Rewrite:

"Hey! I've realized this isn't something I'm interested in, but I wish you the best."

"Thanks for thinking of me, but I need to pass on this."

"I'm being honest with myself about my bandwidth, and I have to say no this time."

"I'm not available for this kind of connection anymore."

✦ Be kind. Be clear. Be done.

Section 5: Prompt — What Would You Do If You Weren't Afraid of Being Called Rude?

The fear of being "rude" has kept more women stuck than failure ever could. It's the leash society uses to keep us in line. But here's a revolutionary thought:

Rude isn't real.

It's code for: "You're making me uncomfortable by telling the truth."

📝 Prompt yourself with this question:

What would I do if I wasn't afraid of being seen as rude?

Examples to spark your fire:

- I'd leave the table when someone made a sexist joke.
- I'd block that guy instead of crafting a "nice" rejection.
- I'd say, "Actually, I don't agree," when everyone else nods.
- I'd quit the group chat that drains my soul.
- I'd speak louder, walk taller, ask for more.

✍️ Write your list. Let it be wild. Let it be honest. Let it be *you* unleashed.

Section 6: Reclaim Your Voice — Say It Without Shrinking

Here's a guide to rewriting your inner (and outer) dialogue with truth and dignity:

Instead of This...	Say This...
"Sorry, just wondering if..."	"Can you clarify this for me?"
"Sorry for bothering you!"	"Thanks for your time."
"I hate to be a pain but…"	"Here's what I need."
"I guess it's fine."	"This doesn't work for me."
"Whatever you want."	"Here's what I prefer."
"I'm probably overreacting but…"	"This doesn't sit right with me, and I'd like to talk about it."
"Just checking in again…"	"Following up. Please confirm."

Your voice is a tool. Stop using it to soothe people who mistreat you. Use it to stand tall in your boundaries and desires.

Section 7: Affirmations for the Truth-Teller

Read these. Out loud. To the mirror. To the walls. To your bones.

- My honesty is not aggression.
- My needs are valid.
- I do not exist to make others comfortable.
- I am not rude—I am real.
- I would rather be disliked for my truth than adored for my silence.
- I do not owe anyone my energy, my time, or my explanation.
- I am learning that peace sometimes requires conflict.
- I don't need to be polite to be powerful.

Section 8: A New Way Forward

You are not here to be palatable. You are not here to be everyone's cup of tea. You are not here to dim, dilute, or disappear to avoid discomfort.

You are here to be **clear**, **brave**, and **truthful**. You are here to choose yourself first.

When E. Jean Carroll stood up and told her truth, she was called "too much," "angry," "crazy." And yet she stood, louder than ever. Because *honesty shakes the room before it heals it.*

So this week, say the thing. Leave the room. Speak up. Disagree. Protect your joy. Offend the people who benefit from your silence. And know that the more honest you become, the freer you will feel.

"Stop asking how to be liked. Start asking how to be real."

— Not My Type Workbook

Chapter 5: Get Out of the Cinderella Business

Theme: Escaping the Fantasy Trap

Introduction: The Fantasy is Failing You

Once upon a time, a perfectly normal girl with ordinary dreams was told that if she stayed sweet, patient, and small enough, a man in shiny shoes would arrive with a glass slipper—and voilà! Her life would begin.

She just had to:

- Tidy up the messes other people left behind.
- Sing through suffering.

- Remain effortlessly beautiful under duress.
- Forgive every betrayal.
- Wait.

This girl was told love would arrive like a parade, that someone would choose her, and that happiness was a reward for compliance. Her name was Cinderella, and she was the original unpaid intern of romance.

We've all been her.

Maybe you weren't sweeping fireplaces, but you were staying in relationships too long. Saying yes to scraps. Being "nice." Hoping your loyalty would be rewarded. Hoping that if you just held on a little longer, *he'd see* you.

But here's the radical truth: **You are not a fairy tale. You are not a fantasy. You are a whole damn force.**

And it's time to quit the Cinderella business for good.

Section 1: Who Sold You the Fantasy?

Before you could even walk, the stories started. Disney, rom-coms, religious scripts, even childhood games—all whispered the same seductive lie:

"One day, someone will come along and complete you."

From Ariel to Bella, from "The Notebook" to *Twilight*, the narrative was clear:

- He'll be brooding.

- You'll be misunderstood.

- There will be drama, longing, sacrifice.

- You'll fix him. He'll redeem you.

- Then everything will finally make sense.

And so you searched for that story. Maybe you're still searching.

But real love isn't a plot twist. It's not fireworks every second. It's not painful or punishing or a puzzle to solve. It's not waiting around to be chosen.

Real love is *not a rescue mission*. It's not something you wait for while your life is on pause.

So let's ask it straight:

- What stories shaped your expectations of love?

- Which ones made you ignore your own needs?

- Which ones made you settle for less than you deserved?

Section 2: Journal Reflection

Prompt: What fairy tale, book, or movie romance shaped your expectations—and harmed you?

📝 Use these guiding questions:

- What did the story teach you about love?

- Who had the power in that story?

- How did it affect your view of dating or relationships?

- What did you internalize that you're still unlearning?

Example:

"I grew up watching *The Little Mermaid*, where Ariel gives up her voice for a man she's never even spoken to. As an adult, I found myself doing the same—silencing my needs, desires, and boundaries just to be 'loved.' I confused losing myself with gaining someone else. That story isn't cute anymore. It's a cautionary tale."

Now you go. Tell the truth. Write the story—and how it tried to write you.

Section 3: Fantasy vs. Reality — A Love Comparison

Let's break the illusion.

This exercise is your **Reality Check List**. On the left, list the qualities of *fantasy love*. On the right, list the *truth of healthy love*. This contrast is everything.

Fantasy Love (What You Were Sold)	Healthy Love (What You Deserve)
Love is chaotic and dramatic	Love is stable, warm, and honest
You should chase or prove yourself	You are met with mutual effort and clarity
If they pull away, it means they care	Emotional availability is not a mystery
Passion = pain	Passion is also safety, consistency, and joy
Jealousy = love	Trust = love
He just needs time, healing, patience	You're not a rehab center
Your worth depends on being chosen	Your worth is non-negotiable and self-sourced

✍ Fill in your own examples. Write the lies you've lived and the truths you're ready to embrace.

This isn't just about relationships—it's about *reprogramming* your emotional blueprint.

Section 4: Why We Cling to the Fantasy

Why do we hold so tightly to illusions?

Because fantasy feels safer than reality.

Fantasy gives us:

- Control: In fantasy, we imagine a version of someone better than they are.
- Hope: It says "someday" things will change—even when they never do.
- Ego protection: If we're chasing a fairy tale, we don't have to admit it's a dead end.

But the problem is—fantasy can't hold you at 3 a.m. It can't communicate. It can't show up. It can't make you feel seen. It can only keep you stuck.

"If someone only loves the fantasy version of you, they don't love *you*. And if you're only in love with their potential, you don't love them—you love a ghost."

Let go of the story. Let reality surprise you.

Section 5: Prompt — What's Better Than Being Chosen?

For centuries, "being chosen" was the gold standard for women. The goal. The prize. The finish line.

But what if that's a scam?

What if the real goal is to:

- **Choose yourself.**
- **Create a life you don't want to be rescued from.**
- **Be *seen*, not selected.**

🏰 Write about this question:

What's better than being chosen?

Examples:

- Being respected.
- Being known for who you are, not how well you perform.
- Choosing *them* back because they've earned it—not because you're desperate to be loved.
- Feeling safe and adored without having to shrink, chase, or prove.

Let your answer burn through the old story. Let it set the new one on fire.

Section 6: Break Up with Your Fantasy

This is your breakup letter—not to a person, but to the fantasy.

📜 **Write a letter like this:**

Dear Fantasy,

I believed in you. I clung to you like a lifeline. You made me think that love had to be epic and exhausting. That if it didn't hurt, it wasn't real. That I wasn't complete without someone else's gaze confirming my worth.

But you lied.

You kept me waiting. You made me betray my own needs. You told me that sacrifice was romantic, and silence was strength. I played the cool girl, the fixer, the dreamer, the muse.

But I'm not playing anymore.

I choose truth over fantasy. I choose myself over being chosen. I choose the messy, beautiful, honest, healing kind of love—the kind I don't have to audition for.

Goodbye, fantasy. I'm not yours anymore.

Love,

Me.

✍ Now you write your own.

Section 7: Stop Waiting—Start Living

If no one ever chooses you, would your life still be rich?

Yes. And here's how you start building that kind of life:

- Make plans that excite you—whether or not you have a date.

- Buy yourself flowers, lingerie, or plane tickets *without a reason.*
- Learn to enjoy your own company. Make yourself laugh.
- Let go of the shame of "singlehood." Being alone is not a failure—it's a flex.
- Create rituals of joy, peace, and pleasure that don't rely on anyone else showing up.

You don't need a prince. You need presence.

"Stop waiting for the doorbell. Build a damn life party and let the doorbell interrupt *you.*"

Section 8: You Are the Main Character Now

This is the part of the movie where the heroine wakes up.

She realizes no one is coming to save her. So she saves herself.

She stops chasing the guy and starts chasing her own joy.

She burns the slipper. She dances barefoot.

She rewrites the ending.

You are not a fantasy.

You are a force.

You are not waiting.

You are becoming.

Conclusion: Happily Ever After Starts Now

Happily ever after isn't a man. It's a moment. A choice. A series of days where you wake up and say:

- I am enough.
- I don't need to be chosen.
- I am the love of my life first.
- I am done performing for scraps.
- I am no longer part of the Cinderella industry.

The fairy tale isn't real. But *you* are.

So take off the glass slipper. Put on combat boots. Or heels. Or nothing. And walk into the rest of your life—unrescued, unbothered, and completely, gloriously free.

"No more waiting. No more wishing. No more wondering.

I'm not your fantasy girl.

I'm the damn plot twist."

— Not My Type Workbook

Absolutely! Here's your **4000-word Chapter 6** of the *Not My Type* workbook by E. Jean Carroll, titled:

Chapter 6: Laugh at the Madness

Theme: Using Humor to Heal Heartbreak

Introduction: If You're Not Laughing, You're Crying

Let's be honest: dating is **insane**.

One minute, you're sipping overpriced cocktails and pretending to care about his fantasy football team, and the next you're spiraling because he watched all your stories but hasn't replied to your text in three days. You've sent a selfie, two "Hey just checking in" texts, and now you're Googling "emotional unavailability vs. narcissism."

We've all been there.

But here's the magic E. Jean Carroll teaches us: when life gets unhinged—**laugh**. Loudly. Boldly. Inappropriately. Not because your heartbreak wasn't real, but because if you don't laugh, you risk getting stuck. Humor is not dismissal—it's defiance. It says, *"This broke me for a minute, but I will not stay broken."*

So welcome to the laugh-out-loud part of your healing. The rom-com montage where you throw popcorn at the screen. The moment you reread old texts and think, "What the hell was I on?" It's time to laugh, snort, cackle, howl—and reclaim the parts of you that were buried under bad dates, worse boyfriends, and tragic "almosts."

Section 1: The Absurdity of Dating Today

Let's take a moment to observe the species known as *modern man on dating apps.*

⬜ **Habitat:** Bumble, Hinge, lurking in DMs.

💬 **Communication Style:** "Hey." (and nothing else)

⬜ **Primary Selfies:** Holding a fish, driving a car, or standing next to a sedated tiger in Thailand.

🎯 **Stated Goals:** "Looking for something real...but not ready for anything serious."

☐ **Favorite Phrase:** "I'm bad at texting."

And we're supposed to find *love* in this mess?

Dating today is like going to a thrift store, hoping to find a diamond ring—but instead, you get mothballs, unmatched socks, and maybe an old vibrator in a Ziplock.

And yet—we survive it. We cry, yes. But then we *laugh*. Because the truth is: nothing heals a tragic love story faster than calling it what it really was—**absolutely ridiculous**.

Section 2: Journal Prompt — Rate the Madness

📝 **List the most ridiculous dating moments you've survived. Then give them a 1–5 rating for comedic value.**

Here's an example table to guide you:

Disaster	What Happened	Comedic Rating (1–5 😂)
"The Polyamory Surprise"	He casually mentioned he had 3 other girlfriends—*after* sleeping with you.	😂😂😂😂😂
"The Ghosting Guru"	He planned your wedding in Week 2, then disappeared forever.	😂😂😂😂
"The Poet"	He sent daily haikus about your boobs.	😂😂😂
"The Momma's Boy"	He FaceTimed you *from his mother's lap.*	😂😂😂😂😂
"The Gym Bro"	He flexed during sex. Not metaphorically. Literally.	😂😂😂

👉 Now fill in your own. Let it be fun. The more cringe, the better. This isn't about shame—it's about **ownership**.

And once you write them out? Read them like you're telling your best friend over wine. Because now that you see it—it's hilarious. And you're still standing.

Section 3: Exercise — Dear Abby (aka, Dear Me)

Here's your next healing ritual: become your own advice columnist.

Take one of your past romantic disasters—the one that had you pacing the kitchen, crying to voicemails, or reading Tarot cards to decode a text—and write a "Dear Abby" letter to yourself, from the version of you who was in the thick of it.

Example:

Dear Abby,

I've been seeing this guy for 4 months. He still hasn't introduced me to his friends, says he's "emotionally overwhelmed," and only texts after 11 PM. But he calls me "baby" and once said I had a magical soul. Is he into me?

— Delusional in Dallas

Now, as your **own wise, hilarious, clear-headed self**, respond like this:

Dear Delusional,

First, thank you for your bravery in writing this letter while submerged in denial. Second, let me be honest: this man is not emotionally overwhelmed—he is emotionally unavailable. He is breadcrumbing you, and calling you "baby" is not a relationship.

Tell him to text one of his other magical-souled women. You deserve a man who texts at *10 AM* and brings you soup when you're sick. Dump him, block him, and book a massage.

— Abby (and your future self who glows)

✍ Now go write your own!

Pick 2 or 3 past disasters. Write the question, then the brutally funny advice. Make it sharp. Make it honest. Make it healing.

Section 4: Prompt — What's Funny Now That Felt Tragic Then?

Here's the wild truth: *most heartbreak is comedy with a time delay.*

What once had you sobbing into your throw pillows is now the funniest thing you tell at brunch.

✍ Write your answer to this prompt:

What's funny now that felt tragic then?

Examples:

- You once bought a whole astrology book to "understand his behavior"—he turned out to be a Capricorn *and* a cheater.

- You cried over a guy who wore cargo shorts in winter.

- You begged someone to love you...who couldn't even spell your name right.

- You planned a birthday party for someone who forgot *your birthday*.

- You once tried to decode a "K" text like it was Morse code for love.

Write it. Relive it. Laugh. That's how the shame dies and power returns.

Section 5: The Healing Power of Humor

Let's get something clear: laughing at your pain doesn't erase it. But it does something better—it **reframes** it.

When you laugh at what broke you, you:

- Take away its power.

- Step out of victimhood and into authorship.

- Signal to the universe that you're moving forward—not because it didn't matter, but because you *do*.

Humor is a boundary. It's a spotlight. It says:

"I see what happened. I survived it. And now I'm putting it in my one-woman comedy special."

So yes, you're allowed to find it funny that he called you his soulmate, then ghosted you after your second pap smear.

That's not bitter. That's *badass*.

Section 6: Flip the Script — From Tragedy to Triumph

✍ Take a breakup, rejection, or failed situationship and rewrite the narrative like a comedy sketch.

Use this format:

- **Title it** like a sitcom episode (e.g., *"The One with the Therapist Who Needed Therapy"*).
- **List the "plot"** like it's bullet points from a stand-up routine.
- **End it with the moral** (the lesson you didn't see then, but you own now).

Example:

Title: "The One with the Deep Texter"

Plot:

- Met on Hinge. Bio said "Emotionally Intelligent" and "Sapiosexual."
- Never FaceTimed. Only sent paragraphs about childhood trauma...at 2 AM.
- Claimed we had a psychic connection. Wouldn't meet in daylight.
- Turned out he was married. His "trauma" was... getting caught.

Moral:

Red flags are not confetti. Trauma doesn't make someone deep—it makes them a candidate for therapy, not a relationship.

✍️ Now you try. Pick a story. Turn it into a sketch. Punchline included.

Section 7: Affirmations for the Light-Hearted Lover

Repeat these in the mirror, in traffic, in the bathroom at weddings:

- I am allowed to laugh at my past.
- I am not embarrassed by my hope—I'm proud of it.
- Every mistake was a lesson in disguise.
- I am a survivor of modern dating—I deserve a medal and a mimosa.
- I don't take rejection personally—I take it as redirection.
- I love the version of me who kept believing.
- I laugh because I lived through it. I laugh because I *own* it.
- I will never cry over cargo shorts again.

Section 8: Close the Chapter with a Toast

🎉 Let's end this chapter with a toast. Raise your metaphorical glass and read aloud:

Here's to every bad date, dead-end text, narcissist, ghoster, gaslighter, and walking ick I ever wasted time on.

Here's to the heartbreak that humbled me—and the humor that healed me.

Here's to the friends who listened, the memes that got me through, and the journal pages soaked in snot and glitter.

Here's to the one who got away—and thank God he did.

Here's to *me*—who never stopped showing up, even when it was hard. Who still believes in love, laughter, and divine timing.

And here's to my next chapter: funnier, freer, and full of actual joy.

Cheers, darling.

Conclusion: Laugh, Then Love Again

Your heartbreaks don't define you. Your laughter does.

You are not broken. You are battle-tested.

You are not foolish. You are fierce.

You are not ashamed. You are hilarious.

So laugh at the madness. Write your punchlines. Tell your story like the comedy queen you are. Because in the end, healing doesn't mean forgetting—it means you can tell the truth and still smile.

"I may not have gotten the guy, but I sure as hell got the material."

— Not My Type Workbook

Chapter 7: Desire Is Not a Dirty Word

Theme: Owning Your Wants Unapologetically

Introduction: Say It Like You Mean It

Let's begin with a revolutionary statement:

Desire is divine.

Not needy. Not shameful. Not dirty. Not "too much."

Desire is the pulse beneath your skin, the electricity in your voice, the reason you're still alive.

And yet—we've been trained to smother it.

From childhood, we were taught that wanting too much—emotionally, sexually, spiritually—made us selfish, dramatic, or ungrateful. Wanting openly was dangerous. Expressing it made you vulnerable. And god forbid you ever demanded more—more love, more attention, more orgasms, more *life*—without apology.

But let's be honest: **the people who told you desire was dangerous were afraid of your power**.

Because nothing is more threatening than a woman who knows what she wants—and asks for it without flinching.

So this chapter is your reckoning. Your reclamation. Your unapologetic YES. To your body. Your voice. Your pleasure. Your purpose.

Because desire is not a distraction.

It's a direction.

And it's time to follow it.

Section 1: The Desire Double Standard

Let's talk about the shame economy.

From the beginning, the rules were different:

- Boys were "curious." Girls were "fast."
- Men were praised for ambition. Women were told they were "too much."
- He wants sex? Normal.

You want sex? *Thirsty.*

- He wants commitment? A catch.

You want commitment? *Desperate.*

Women are taught to want only after they've made sure everyone else is comfortable. Only after we've earned it. Only if we've proven we're "not like the other girls."

Enough.

We were not born to be polite about pleasure.

We were not built to suppress hunger.

We were not created to live on crumbs.

So today, we name the wants that never got spoken. We unlock the rooms where we've hidden our hunger. And we let desire be holy again.

Section 2: Journal Reflection

Prompt: What have you been ashamed to want—emotionally, sexually, spiritually?

✍ Write your answers without editing, apologizing, or justifying. Make it a confession, a celebration, a declaration.

Break it down into three categories:

💜 *Emotionally:*

- I want to be adored without having to earn it.
- I want someone to ask how I am and actually mean it.
- I want consistency, not intensity that disappears.

🔥 *Sexually:*

- I want to feel powerful, not performative.
- I want to ask for what I want in bed without feeling "extra."
- I want partners who celebrate my pleasure, not just tolerate it.

🌀 *Spiritually:*

- I want to feel connected to something bigger than pain.
- I want rituals, joy, magic—without having to subscribe to anyone's dogma.
- I want a life that turns me on, in every sense.

Now go back and highlight the ones that make you squirm. Those are your keys.

Your shame is the gatekeeper. Your desire is the guide.

Section 3: Exercise — Your Desire Map

This is not just about sex.

This is about what **turns you on** about life.

✍ Draw or list your **Desire Map**—the parts of life that light your fire, wake your senses, make you feel most alive.

Use these prompts:

Category	What Turns Me On
Sensory (touch, taste, smell)	Velvet sheets, ripe mango, the smell of cedar, silk on skin
Emotional	Feeling seen, deep conversations, uncontrollable laughter
Creative	Writing raw truths, making playlists, building something from nothing
Spiritual	Candlelight rituals, full moon walks, honest prayer
Physical	Dancing alone, yoga at sunrise, being kissed like a promise
Romantic	Eye contact that doesn't flinch, forehead kisses, slow mornings in bed

Let it be sacred. Let it be silly. Let it be *you*.

Now look at your map. This is not a fantasy—it's a roadmap. A blueprint. An invitation.

Start following it.

Section 4: Who Benefits When You Shrink Your Desires?

Spoiler: Not you.

Every time you silence your want to avoid "drama," to stay "chill," to seem "low maintenance," someone else gets the upper hand.

Someone else stays comfortable while you contort.

This is your reminder:

- Desire is not manipulation.
- Wanting more is not ungrateful.
- Being direct is not demanding.
- Being sexual is not an invitation to be objectified.

When women shrink their wants, the world gets smaller.

Your hunger expands the universe. Your honesty makes things bloom. Your full-bodied YES is how the world changes.

Section 5: Prompt — How Would You Live if Your Needs Were Sacred?

Take a breath and imagine this:

You never again apologized for needing reassurance.

You never again explained why touch matters to you.

You never again asked for permission to speak your truth.

You never again felt guilty for wanting *more*—attention, affection, freedom, orgasms, quiet.

✍ Write your answer to this journal prompt:

If I believed my needs were sacred, I would...

Examples:

- Stop shrinking my texts to seem less "needy."
- Tell my partner what turns me on instead of hoping they'll guess.
- Ask for space when I'm overwhelmed.
- Say "no" without rehearsing a justification.
- Stop calling myself high maintenance just because I have standards.
- End things with people who make me feel like a burden.

Sacred doesn't mean fragile. It means *honored*.

Start honoring what you need.

Section 6: Say It—Without Apology

You're allowed to say what you want. You're allowed to claim what feeds your soul.

Let's practice rewriting some common hesitations into sacred affirmations:

Instead of This...	Say This...
"Sorry, but I'd really like..."	"Here's what I need."

"I don't want to be a bother, but…"	"This matters to me."
"I hope this isn't too much to ask..."	"I expect this in my relationships."
"I don't usually do this but…"	"This is part of who I am."
"I know this might sound weird but…"	"This brings me pleasure."

Make a list of 5 things you want—small or large.

Then rewrite them as if they were **non-negotiables**, because they are.

Section 7: Sacred Wants, Sacred Standards

Here's what sacred desire looks like in real life:

- You tell a lover how to touch you *before* they do it wrong.
- You don't settle for half-relationships, "situationships," or guessing games.
- You stop pretending cuddling is enough when you're craving commitment.
- You don't fake orgasms. You don't fake interest. You don't fake fine.
- You light candles *for yourself.* You buy lingerie *for yourself.* You ask God *directly* what you need.

When desire becomes sacred, you stop bargaining.

You stop bending.

You stop being grateful for crumbs.

And instead, you feast.

Section 8: Mirror Work — I Am Allowed to Want

Go to a mirror. Lock eyes with yourself. Say these out loud:

- "My wants are not embarrassing—they're essential."
- "Desire lives in me. It is not borrowed, stolen, or conditional."
- "I am not hard to love. I am hard to manipulate."
- "I do not apologize for hungers that make me more alive."
- "I am not waiting to be picked. I am choosing me."
- "I am allowed to take up space—in the bedroom, at the table, and in my own heart."

Repeat until the cringe turns to courage.

Repeat until your voice doesn't shake.

Repeat until you believe it.

Section 9: Reclamation Ritual — Light Your Want on Fire

🔥 Here's your final ritual for this chapter:

Write down a desire you've suppressed—emotional, sexual, spiritual.

Then do one of the following:

- Say it aloud in the mirror.
- Burn the paper (safely!) and say, "This belongs to me now."
- Text it to someone who needs to hear it.

- Write it on your body with lipstick or eyeliner.

This is symbolic, but sacred. You are lighting up your own permission.

Conclusion: Desire Is How You Return to Yourself

You were never meant to be small, muted, or polite about your joy.

You were born with a compass in your chest that points directly toward your wholeness. It's called desire.

Desire wakes you up.

Desire guides you home.

Desire says, "This is what it feels like to be *alive.*"

So let the world call you selfish.

Let them call you dramatic.

Let them call you high-maintenance.

Because the truth is—you are not "too much."

You are finally giving yourself *enough.*

"Want it. Name it. Claim it.

Because what you desire isn't too big—it's *sacred.*"

— Not My Type Workbook

Absolutely! Here's your **4000-word Chapter 8** for the *Not My Type* workbook by E. Jean Carroll, titled:

Chapter 8: The Comeback Is the Plot Twist

Theme: Reinventing Yourself Post-Heartbreak

Introduction: This Is Your Plot Twist Moment

Heartbreak has a smell. A sound. A shape. It wraps around your throat like smoke and turns your mirror into a battlefield. It whispers: *"You lost. You failed. You'll never feel whole again."*

But heartbreak is a liar.

Because the truth is, heartbreak is not the end.

It's the goddamn ignition.

Welcome to your plot twist.

This chapter isn't about crawling back.

It's about bursting forward.

It's about becoming the kind of woman who thanks the heartbreak for waking her up.

This is your post-breakup glow-up. Your phoenix moment. Your wild return to yourself. Because the comeback is not polite. It doesn't ask for permission. It rips off the script and writes a brand new scene.

So get ready. You're not healing quietly.

You're healing **loudly**.

With glitter. With fire. With new boundaries and hotter selfies.

You're not who you were before the heartbreak.

You're **better**.

Section 1: The False Ending Myth

Movies lie.

They show you two people kissing in the rain, cue the swelling music, and roll the credits. But in real life, heartbreak is where the movie *begins*.

Breakups don't mean you failed.

They mean you learned.

They mean you dared.

They mean you're alive.

You didn't lose love. You outgrew a chapter. You leveled up. You stopped pretending. You got honest about what no longer fit. That isn't failure. That's evolution.

"The end of a love story is not the end of *your* story. It's the start of a better one."

So stop reading your life like a tragedy. You're not Juliet. You're the damn director.

Section 2: Journal Prompt — What Version of Yourself Is Ready to Be Reborn?

✍ Answer the following honestly and fiercely:

- What beliefs about love am I leaving behind?
- What parts of me were dimmed in that relationship?
- What am I no longer tolerating—from others, from myself?
- What qualities were buried beneath survival?
- What kind of woman do I want to meet in the mirror next?

Now write a name for her. A title. A vibe. An aesthetic.

She is not a fantasy—she's your next chapter.

Examples:

- The Unbothered Flame
- Boundaries & Body Oil
- The Softest Savage
- The Woman Who Doesn't Text First
- She Who Laughs in Red Lipstick

Name her. Step into her. She's already inside you.

Section 3: Breakup Ritual — Burn the Past, Baby

You've cried enough. Now we *ceremonialize* it.

☐☐ **Create a breakup ritual to seal the past and reclaim your power.**

Instructions:

1. **Choose your elements:** Candle, music, a letter, photos, incense, journal, bath, glitter—whatever feels sacred or wild.

2. **Write a goodbye letter** to the relationship, not the person.

3. **Say these words (or your own):**

"This chapter taught me. This chapter grew me. This chapter is closed."

4. **Burn it, bury it, soak it, shred it.**

Let it go with flair. With fire. With *style*.

5. **Do something pleasurable after.**

Cook something decadent. Put on music. Dance. Kiss your own shoulder.

This isn't a funeral. It's a rebirth.

Section 4: The Glow-Up Isn't Just Physical—It's Spiritual

Sure, you can cut your hair, buy lingerie, and hit the gym—and yes, do all of that. But the real glow-up is internal.

It's when:

- You stop stalking their socials and start stalking your dreams.
- You make peace with your reflection.
- You reclaim your mornings.

- You flirt with your future instead of your ex.

✦ Here's your **Spiritual Glow-Up Checklist**:

Reclaim This	Practice
Time	Create a morning ritual that starts with *you*—no phone, no noise.
Space	Redecorate your room. Move the bed. Burn new scents. Shift the vibe.
Energy	Detox your digital life. Unfollow, mute, block. Make it sacred.
Voice	Start saying what you mean, not what keeps the peace.
Desire	Make a new list of what turns you on—emotionally, physically, creatively.
Power	Make choices like someone who's already loved—because you are.

👑 Choose three of these to begin this week. Declare it your comeback initiation.

Section 5: Prompt — What Does Freedom Feel Like, and How Will You Celebrate It?

This is the chapter where you don't just feel free—you *act* like it.

👑 Journal your truth:

- What did I mistake for love that was really control?
- What weight have I dropped now that they're gone?
- What do I get to do *now* that I couldn't before?
- What does freedom feel like in my body, my breath, my soul?
- What ritual or act will I do to celebrate this freedom?

Examples:

- Take yourself to a solo dinner and toast to your own damn heart.

- Plan a trip to a place that makes you feel untouchable.

- Host a Breakup Brunch with champagne and glitter and everyone you trust.

- Write your name on your bedroom mirror in lipstick.

Celebrate like your life just reopened—because it did.

Section 6: Affirmations for the Comeback Queen

Repeat these like you believe them—even before you do. Say them into the mirror, in the bath, on a walk, after a cry.

- My heart broke—but it also bloomed.

- I am not my past. I am my *power*.

- I am the plot twist I've been waiting for.

- This is not a setback—it's a setup.

- I do not chase. I attract.

- I thank the lesson and bless the release.

- I am not rebuilding. I am rebirthing.

- The version of me that's coming? *She's unstoppable.*

Make one of these your phone background. Make another your morning mantra.

Section 7: Rebuild Your Love Story (With You as the Lead)

Breakups make space. Don't fill it with scraps. Fill it with *yourself.*

🐾 Try this visualization:

Imagine your life six months from now—fully healed, fully glowing.

- Where are you waking up?
- What does your body feel like?
- Who are you texting *less*?
- What are you saying "yes" to?
- What music plays as you walk down the street like the main character?
- Who did you become?

Write it like it's already true.

Example:

"I wake up with sunlight on my skin and no anxiety in my chest. My phone is quiet, and it feels good. I'm not waiting for a message—I'm waiting for nothing. My closet looks like a woman who knows her worth. My playlist is half Beyoncé, half Nina Simone. I feel free. I feel gorgeous. I feel *mine.*"

Now it's your turn.

Section 8: The Comeback Code — What You Now Refuse to Forget

This isn't just healing—it's strategy. You're not going back to who you were. She got you here. But she's not the final form.

Write your **Comeback Code.** These are the commandments of your new life. Tape them to your mirror. Tattoo them in your soul.

📝 Your Comeback Code might include:

- I will never again beg for love.
- I trust how I feel, even when no one else validates it.
- If it costs my peace, it's too expensive.
- My energy is not up for debate.
- I will not settle for potential.
- I date with my eyes open and my boundaries intact.
- I don't explain my standards. I embody them.
- I am *no one's* lesson. I am my own reward.

Now write 3–5 of your own.

Section 9: Final Ritual — Declare Your Plot Twist

This is it. The last step. The exorcism. The epilogue.

Declare your comeback. Write a letter. A toast. A manifesto. It's for no one else but you.

📜 Example:

"To the girl I was when he left—thank you.

You cried with grace. You felt it all.

But now, your job is done.

A new woman is here.

She laughs more. Sleeps better. Expects joy.

She's not waiting for closure. She *is* the closing act.

This is my plot twist. This is my power.

This is my freedom.

And I will never be the same."

📝 Now write yours. Speak it aloud. Frame it. Burn it. Sing it. Whatever you do—
own it.

Conclusion: The Woman You Became

Let's be clear: this workbook never promised you a man.

It promised you something better.

Yourself.

The woman you became after the heartbreak? She's a marvel.

She doesn't chase. She *chooses*.

She doesn't settle. She *soars*.

She doesn't shrink. She *shines*.

She is the plot twist.

She is the freedom.

She is the love story.

And anyone who meets her now? They better come correct—because she's not available for anything less than extraordinary.

"The heartbreak was real. But so is the rebirth."

—Not My Type Workbook

Made in United States
Orlando, FL
03 July 2025

62623183R00039